THE ALL NEW
ELEPHANT JAM

A COLLECTION OF
OLD SONGS, NEW SONGS,
POP SONGS, MOM SONGS,
PARTNER SONGS, PAL SONGS,
MAD, SAD AND GLAD SONGS,
SUMMER, SPRING AND FALL SONGS,
BIG, LITTLE, SMALL SONGS,
SONGS FOR FINGERS, HANDS AND TOES,
EYES AND EARS AND MOUTH AND NOSE,
RHYMES FOR COUNTING, RHYMES FOR CHOOSING,
MORNING, NIGHT OR AFTERNOON-ZING,
TUNES TO WHISTLE, PLAY OR HUM,
BY YOURSELF OR WITH A CHUM,
SO HOOT AND HOLLER, TOOT AND BAM,
AND HAVE YOURSELF AN «ELEPHANT JAM»

...WITH LOVE FROM SHARON, LOIS & BRAM

Sharon, Lois & Bram

THE ALL NEW

ELEPHANT JAM

ILLUSTRATED BY DAVID SHAW

A LORRAINE GREEY BOOK

CROWN PUBLISHERS, INC.
NEW YORK

Dedication

To the music makers—the children and adults at work and play, in their homes and classrooms, in city streets and country lanes, through the days and into the nights, across the land and over the sea—to all of you who have touched our lives with your songs, we gratefully dedicate this book.

· ♥ · ♥ · ♥ · ♥ · ♥ · ♥ · ♥ · ♥ · ♥ · ♥ · ♥ · ♥ · ♥ ·

Acknowledgements

This book owes much to many people: to the teachers and children who, though our many years of work in schools, have helped shape our ideas of how music and children should come together; to our colleagues, who have given freely of repertoire, skills and insights; and to the folk community, who provided the inspiration and support for the passing on of a special kind of music that we cherish.

Thanks to David Shaw, who designed and illustrated the book, cover to cover, and astonished us with the number of ways he could discover to tell a story; to Molly Thom, who, in many creative projects such as this, is the fourth member of the trio. Our families, who are always there in all that we do, are part of this book, too.

And finally, we salute our audience, whose enthusiasm and encouragement have been an inspiration to us since we first stepped on stage.

To you all, our very deepest thanks.

Sharon, Lois and Bram

· ♥ · ♥ · ♥ · ♥ · ♥ · ♥ · ♥ · ♥ · ♥ · ♥ · ♥ · ♥ · ♥ ·

Text and Musical Arrangements © 1989 Elephant Records Inc. This book is a revised and expanded edition of *Elephant Jam* © 1980 by Pachyderm Music. Illustrations © 1989 David Shaw.

The music credits appearing on page 128 are herewith made a part of this copyright page.

Published in 1989 in the United States by Crown Publishers, Inc.
225 Park Avenue South
New York, New York 10003

Originally published in Canada by McGraw-Hill Ryerson, Ltd.

CROWN is a trademark of Crown Publishers, Inc.

Manufactured in Canada

Library of Congress Cataloguing-in-Publication Data

Elephant jam.
   Piano and guitar arrangements of folksongs, playground chants, and singing games.
   Eighty-two songs and games from the Canadian authors'/musical group's original songbook and from their concerts and television show "The Elephant Show." Includes illustrations and game instructions.
   1. Children's songs.   2. Singing games.
[1. Songs.   2. Singing games.   3. Games.]
I. Sharon, Lois, and Bram.
M1992.E39   1989   89-750476

ISBN 0-517-57377-6

First Crown Edition   0 9 8 7 6 5 4 3 2 1

Cover photograph by Gordon Hay

**Produced by
Lorraine Greey Publications Limited
56 The Esplanade, Suite 303
Toronto, Ontario M5E 1A7**

Contents

Guitar and Ukulele Chords

Here are diagrams for the most common chords in this book. For chords that do not appear on this page, please consult a more complete guitar or ukulele book.

Diminished Chords

There are only three diminished chords (and their inversions). Any diminished chord, no matter what its note name, can be played by one of the following:

The chord can take its name from any one of the four notes in it.

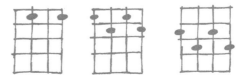

6

Introduction

Someone once asked Woody Guthrie, "What is a children's song?" Woody replied, "Any song kids like to sing." If you should ask us, "What's a grown-up song?" Like Woody, we'd say, "Any song grown-ups like to sing."

That's what *Elephant Jam* is all about—songs for everyone who likes to sing and play about everything under the sun. We gathered these songs, rhymes and games from everywhere and everyone, and now, wherever we go, we hear kids and grown-ups singing them, dancing and laughing, alone and together. Making music. Having fun.

This book is a collection of "kids'/grown-up" songs and games, most of which are selected from our first four albums. In this revised edition, we have changed the format for explaining game and action songs to make them easier to understand; eliminated some activities to make room for new ones; and added new piano arrangements. We've also included—for the first time **ever**—a neat arrangement by Eddie Graf of "Skinnamarink" for "four hands on one piano"!

The purpose of the book has not changed: to convey the spirit of each song as clearly as possible through music, illustrations and text in the hope that these will serve as a starting point for exploring new ideas. The tunes have symbols for chordal players, and we've added chord diagrams specifically for guitar and ukulele players. The piano arrangements are geared for beginning and intermediate students, and they are intended to reflect the mood of the songs as they appear on our recordings.

We've been making music, alone and together, for more than 25 years, and the songs in *Elephant Jam* have been our friends during this time. It's quite simple: a good song—true and fine and sweetly sung—gives pleasure to all, always.

Sharon Lois & Bram

THROUGHOUT THIS BOOK YOU'LL FIND THESE SYMBOLS. THEY WILL TELL YOU AT A GLANCE HOW TO ARRANGE YOURSELVES WHEN PLAYING A GAME.

SIT AT RANDOM

SIT IN A CIRCLE

STAND AT RANDOM

STAND IN A CIRCLE

STAND IN A CIRCLE WITH ONE CHILD IN THE MIDDLE

STAND IN A CIRCLE WITH ONE CHILD ON THE OUTSIDE

PARTNER GAME

Elephant Rhyme

The elephant goes like this and that,

STRETCH!

He's terribly big

And he's terribly fat;

wiggle your fingers...

He has no fingers,

He has no toes,

swing your trunk!

But, goodness gracious, what a nose!

One Elephant, Deux Éléphants

Children all over the world sing this song in their own language while they play this game — trunks linked to tails — with great delight. To us it seems the sweetest music this side of childhood!

Singing game

Moderately

mf pesante

1. One el-e-phant went out to play, up-on a spi-der's web one day. He had such e-nor-mous fun that he called for an-oth-er el-e-phant to come.

left to come.

2. Deux éléphants allaient jouer
   Sur une toile d'araignée.
   Ils s'amusaient tellement bien
   Qu'ils appelaient à un autre, viens!

3. Three elephants went out to play
   Upon a spider's web one day.
   They had such enormous fun
   That they called for another elephant to come.

4. Quatre éléphants allaient jouer
   Sur une toile d'araignée.
   Ils s'amusaient tellement bien
   Qu'ils appelaient à un autre, viens!

5. All the elephants were out at play
   Upon a spider's web one day.
   They had such enormous fun
   But there were no more elephants left to come.

How to play:
Choose one person to be the first elephant, with the rest of the "herd" sitting on the floor. At the end of each verse, add another elephant until there are no more elephants to come. With a large group, add more than one elephant at a time.

9

Everyone Gather 'Round
Songs for Singing

It seems that the newest crop of kids—say within the past five years or so—is probably the singingest bunch we've known since before the days of records and TV. Ditto for parents. We've read about the good old days, when making music was the *only* family entertainment, when the song was a family treasure and playing an instrument was as natural as eating and sleeping. But we never experienced those times ourselves. What we know now is that because of the generous availability of good music for kids, the simple delight of singing a good song, when and where and how you like, is once more a natural and pleasing thing to do. Everything old is new again. And here are some old songs—and new ones, too—to start you singing "till the day is done."

Hey Dum Diddeley Dum

This song, with its nonsense chorus, is one of our favorite sing-along songs; in fact, it is often an encore in our concerts. What a pretty sight it is to see families arm in arm, swaying from side to side, everyone singing together "till the day is done."

Music and lyrics by Marc Stone

we just found this brand-new sound, It's a hey dum did-de-ley dum.

2. Come join in the fun,
   With a hey dum diddeley dum.
   We're gonna sing till the day is done,
   Hey dum diddeley dum.
   Chorus

3. Everyone come and sing,
   With a hey dum diddeley dum.
   We're gonna make these old rafters ring with
       our
   Hey dum diddeley dum.
   Chorus

You can make up your own verses, like this:

Time to say so long,
With a hey dum diddeley dum.
Can't stop singing this ol' song,
Hey dum diddeley dum.

Jenny Jenkins

Here's a tongue-twisting, color-rhyming song. In case you're wondering what the "polly wolly, tiddle taddle" part means, it is the same as "E, I, E, I, O" in *Old MacDonald* — sheer nonsense.

Color song

1. Oh, will you wear red, oh, my dear, oh, my dear, oh, will you wear red, Jen-ny Jenk-ins? No, I won't wear red, I'd rath-er soak my head. Gon-na find me a pol-ly wol-ly, tid-dle tad-dle, seek-a dou-ble, use-a cause-a roll-a find me, Roll,_____ Jen-ny Jenk-ins,

2. Oh, will you wear blue, oh, my dear, oh,
   my dear,
   Oh, will you wear blue, Jenny Jenkins?
   No, I won't wear blue, rather eat my shoe.
   Chorus

3. Oh, will you wear green, oh, my dear, oh,
   my dear,
   Oh, will you wear green, Jenny Jenkins?
   No, I won't wear green, ain't fit to be seen.
   Chorus

4. Oh, will you wear navy, oh, my dear, oh,
   my dear,
   Oh, will you wear navy, Jenny Jenkins?
   No, I won't wear navy, rather swim in gravy.
   Chorus

5. Then what will you wear, oh, my dear, oh,
   my dear,
   Then what will you wear, Jenny Jenkins?
   Well, I'll just go bare, with a ribbon in my
   hair.
   Chorus

You can put any color you like into this song. Some colors are more difficult to find rhymes for than others. For example, the best we can find for orange is ''door hinge''! Remember to stand up if you're wearing the color mentioned in the rhyme.

Riding Along (Singing a Cowboy Song)

This junior cowboy song evokes a sense of the bond between an ol' cowpoke and his trusty steed — at once his partner and loyal friend.

Words and music by Margaret I. Fletcher and Margaret C. Denison

With a lope

Rid-ing a- long, sing-ing a cow-boy song, Rid-ing a- long, Sing-ing a song. O-LEE- O - LEE O-LEE- O- LAY O - LEE - O - LAY.

1. My boots are made of leath-er and I have a cow-boy hat. I've got my hols-ter tied down and I have a la - ri-at. I climb in-to the sad-dle and I start out on the trail,

2. My pony is a beauty, his name is Buckaroo,
   Whatever I may ask him he will know just
     what to do.
   He'll canter oh so slowly or he'll gallop like
     the wind.
   O-LEE-O-LAY.

   Chorus

3. We have to guard the cattle ev'ry minute of
     the day,
   And be most awfully careful not to let them
     run away.
   So 'round and 'round, up in the air, I twirl
     my lariat,
   O-LEE-O-LAY.

   Chorus

4. We'll ride across the prairie till we see the
     setting sun,
   Then come back to the bunkhouse after all
     our work is done.
   To beefsteak for my supper and some hay for
     Buckaroo,
   O-LEE-O-LAY.

   Chorus

Matthew, Mark, Luke and John

Much of the fun of singing this extended round (with its three distinct melodies) lies in the contrast between the mock seriousness of the tunes and the plain silliness of the story.

Stately

3 - part round

① Mat - thew, Mark, Luke and John, went to bed with their brit - ches on.

John got up in the mid-dle of the night, and said his brit - ches were too tight.

② Mat - thew, Ma - ark, Luke and John went to bed with their

brit - ches__ on, ③ John got up in the mid-dle, in the mid-dle of the night, and

said his brit-ches, said his brit-ches were too tight. John got up in the mid-dle, in the

mid-dle of the night and said his brit-ches were too tight.

All Hid

We first heard this call-and-response song from Leon Bibb at the Vancouver Children's Festival.

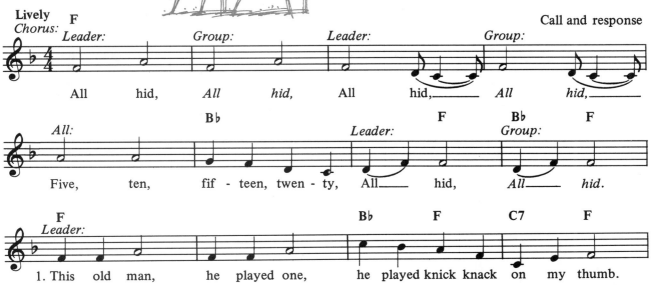

Lively
Chorus:

Leader: All hid, *Group: All hid,* *Leader:* All hid,_____ *Group: All hid,_____*

All: Five, ten, fif-teen, twen-ty, *Leader:* All_____ hid, *Group: All_____ hid.*

Leader: 1. This old man, he played one, he played knick knack on my thumb.

Knick knack, pad-dy-whack give your dog a bone,— This old man came rol-ling home.

Use any 4-line poem for the verses. Here are some suggestions:

Horse and a flea and the three blind mice
Sat on a curbstone, shootin' dice.
Horse he slipped and fell on the flea.
Whoops, said the flea, there's a horse on
    me!
(from: *Boom, Boom, Ain't It Great To Be
    Crazy*)

One elephant went out to play
Upon a spider's web one day.
He had such enormous fun
That he called for another elephant to come.

You can make other new verses to *All Hid* by taking familiar verses and dropping them into the melody. Some others to try: *Shortnin' Bread* and *Turkey in the Straw*.

The Very Best Band

When we were planning our third record, *Singing 'n Swinging*, we thought it would be neat to sing a song about the guys who play in the band. Sharon's husband, Joe, came up with this marching song with five different tunes, all about the grandest band in all the land.

Music and lyrics by Joe Hampson
Partner song

March ①
Chorus:
We have a band,_____ the ver-y best band_____ in all the land, in all the land, in all the land. We have a land._____

Tuba ②
We have a tu - ba, tu - ba, tu - ba, tu - ba, tu - ba, tu - ba, tu - ba, too. We have a tu - ba, too.

How to play:

Divide into five groups, or just sing with four friends. Start with the "very best band" tune, and all sing it through twice. Group 1 keeps singing the chorus; each group adds, one at a time, its own part, starting with the tuba, then the trombone, trumpet and, finally, the piccolo. In the end, all five groups sing their parts together.

She'll Be Comin' 'Round the Mountain

To quote Alan Lomax (*Folk Songs of North America*), ''this early western railroad ditty... catches the jubilation of that halcyon day when the first steam engine came whistling and snorting into a horse-and-buggy town on the prairies.'' Ya-hoo!

Action song

Brightly

1. She'll be com-in' 'round the moun-tain when she comes. *Toot, toot.* She'll be com-in' 'round the moun-tain when she comes. *Toot, toot.* She'll be com-in' 'round the moun-tain, she'll be com-in' 'round the moun-tain, She'll be com-in' 'round the moun-tain when she comes. *Toot, toot!* 2. She'll be comes. *Whoa back, toot,*

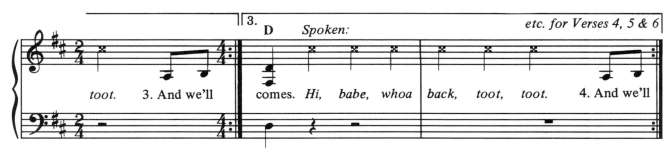

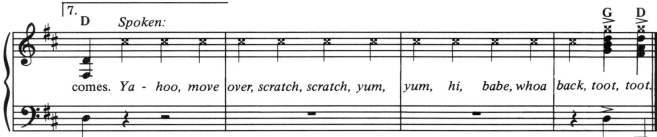

2. She'll be driving six white horses when she comes *Whoa back…*

5. She'll be wearin' red pajamas when she comes *Scratch, scratch…*

3. And we'll all go out to meet her when she comes *Hi, babe…*

6. And she'll have to sleep with Grandma when she comes *Move over…*

4. And we'll all have chicken and dumplings when she comes *Yum, yum…*

7. And we'll have a great big party when she comes *Ya-hoo…*

Fish and Chips

This camp song is really three different tunes that sound great when sung together — we call songs like this "partner songs." It's a simple way to start singing in harmony. Listen to your own song with one ear and to the blending of all the songs with the other.

How to play:
Divide the singers into three groups. The first group starts with tune 1; when they start it a second time, group 2 begins tune 2. Next time around, group 3 starts tune 3. This means group 1 sings its tune three times, group 2 twice, and group 3 once. After everyone knows all the tunes, each single group can sing all three tunes in order, starting one group after the other.

Bye 'n' Bye

This simple spiritual was sung in the state of Texas more than 100 years ago. Lying in bed and counting stars through your window was a nice way to fall asleep and dream sweet dreams — and it still is.

Slowly

Spiritual

Cmaj7   **Fmaj7**   **Cmaj7**   **C6**

Stars shin - ing num - ber, num-ber one, num - ber two, num - ber three, good

mp

Fmaj7   **Cmaj7**   **Dm7**   **Cmaj7**   **C6**   **Fmaj7**

Lord.   Bye 'n' bye, bye 'n' bye, good   Lord.   Bye 'n'

Cmaj7   1. 2. **Fmaj7**   3. **Fmaj7**   **Cmaj7**

bye,   bye 'n' bye.   bye,   bye 'n' bye.

ritard. e dim.   *p*

2. Stars shining number, number four,
   Number five, number six, good Lord.
   Bye 'n' bye, bye 'n' bye, good Lord.
   Bye 'n' bye, bye 'n' bye.

3. Stars shining number, number seven,
   Number eight, number nine, good Lord.
   Bye 'n' bye, bye 'n' bye, good Lord.
   Bye 'n' bye, bye 'n' bye, bye 'n' bye.

25

Candy Man, Salty Dog

This song has been a great favorite of all the children — from "junior kindergartners" to "junior high-ers" — with whom we have sung it during the past twenty years.

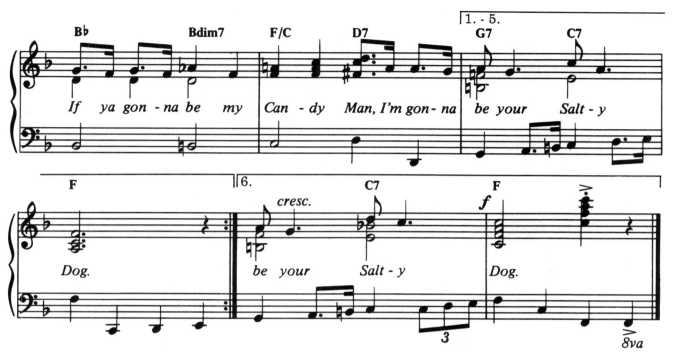

If ya gon-na be my Can-dy Man, I'm gon-na be your Salt-y Dog.

be your Salt-y Dog.

2. Little red light, *Little red light,*
   Little green light, *Little green light,*   3x
   Stop on the red and go on the green,
   Don't mess with Mister In-Between.   2x

3. Gingerbread Man, *Gingerbread Man,*   3x
   Santa Claus, *Santa Claus,*
   Gingerbread Man with the raisins for your
        eyes,
   Gonna eat you quick as I can.   2x

4. I got a peppermint stick, *got a peppermint
        stick*
   And a little brass band, *and a little brass*   3x
        band,
   And I'd do anything in this whole wide world,
   Just to get my Candy Man back.   2x

5. Cantaloupe, *Cantaloupe,*   3x
   Honeydew, *Honeydew,*
   Can't elope tonight, Dad's got the car,
   But, Honey, do marry me.   2x

6. *Repeat verse 1.*

After singing this song through "straight,"
sing the lines and verses in high falsetto,
low basso, in accents or with any special
effects you can invent.

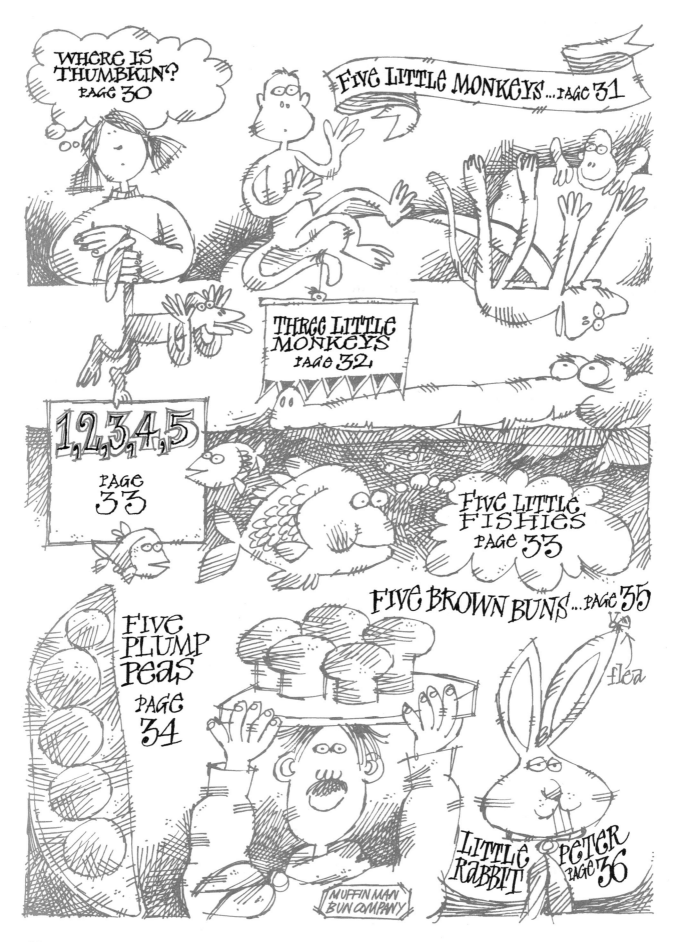

Where is Thumbkin?
Finger Plays

"Finger Plays" are simple poems or ditties where the fingers help tell the story. They speak of ordinary things—naming fingers or counting sweets or making animals—and that is their charm. Helping a toddler find "thumbkin," "ring ma'am" and "pinky," and then putting them together to make a rabbit is the sweetest way to start a rabbit song—and don't think for a moment that big kids don't enjoy a good rabbit tale, too!

THERE WAS A LITTLE MAN PAGE 38

CABIN IN THE WOOD PAGE 39

ARABELLA MILLER PAGE 37

Where is Thumbkin?

Perhaps the definitive finger-naming rhyme of all — and the dearest. We particularly love this song in concert when the littles and the grown-ups together, with pinkies held high, respond, ''Here I am, here I am...''

Gently

Echo rhyme

Where is Thumb-kin, *where is Thumb-kin?* Here I am, *Here I am.*

How are you this morn-ing? *Ver-y well I thank you.* Run and hide, *Run and hide.*

2. Where is pointer, *where is pointer?...*

3. Where is middle man, *where is middle man?...*

4. Where is ring, ma'am, *where is ring, ma'am?...*

5. Where is pinky, *where is pinky?...*

6. Where's the whole family, *where's the whole family?...* (2x)
Here we are, *here we are.* (2x)

Five Little Monkeys

In our concerts, whenever we put up five fingers for the monkeys and one palm for the bed the audience just takes off on its own.

Emphasize the boldfaced words or syllables.

Five little **mon**keys **jump**ing on the **bed**.

One fell **off** and **bumped** his **head**.

Mama called the **doc**tor, the **doc**tor **said**:

"**No more monkeys jumping on the bed!**"

Four little **mon**keys **jump**ing on the **bed**.
One fell **off** and **bumped** her **head**.
Mama called the **doc**tor, the **doc**tor **said**:
"**No more monkeys jumping on the bed!**"

Three little **mon**keys **jump**ing on the **bed**.
One fell **off** and **bumped** his **head**.
Mama called the **doc**tor, the **doc**tor **said**:
"**No more monkeys jumping on the bed!**"

Two little **mon**keys **jump**ing on the **bed**.
One fell **off** and **bumped** her **head**.
Mama called the **doc**tor, the **doc**tor **said**:
"**No more monkeys jumping on the bed!**"

One little **mon**key **jump**ing on the **bed**.
One fell **off** and **bumped** his **head**.
Mama called the **doc**tor, the **doc**tor **said**:
"**No more monkeys jumping on the bed!**"

No more **mon**keys **jump**ing on the **bed**.
None fell **off** and **bumped** their **heads**.
Mama called the **doc**tor, the **doc**tor **said**:
"**Put those monkeys right to bed!**"

Three Little Monkeys

When the five little monkeys finally went to bed, they might have had a dream like this about their cousins in the jungle.

Emphasize the boldfaced words or syllables of this rhythmic chant.

Three little **mon**keys
Swinging in a **tree**.

Along came a **croc**odile,

As **quiet** as can **be**.

The **first** monkey **said**,
"You **can't** catch **me**!"

SNAP!

Two little **mon**keys
Swinging in a **tree**.
Along came a **croc**odile,
As **quiet** as can **be**.
The **sec**ond monkey **said**,
"You **can't** catch **me**!"
SNAP!

One little **mon**key
Swinging in a **tree**.
Along came a **croc**odile,
As **quiet** as can **be**.
The **last** monkey **said**,
"You **can't** catch **me**!"
SNAP!

"Missed me!"

Here's another version:

Three little **mon**keys
Swinging in a **tree**.
Teasing Mr. **Al**ligator,
"**Can't** catch **me**!"
SNAP!...

Here are two fishy rhymes for the wee babies.

1,2,3,4,5

Moderately

Country rhyme

F   Gm7   C7

One, two, three, four, five, once I caught a fish a - live;

Gm7   C7   Bb   C7   F

Six, sev - en, eight, nine, ten, then I let it go a - gain.

F   Cdim   Gm7   C7

Why did you let it go? Be - cause it bit my fin - ger so.

Gm7   C7   Gm7   C7   F

Which fin - ger did it bite? This lit - tle fin - ger on the right.

Five Little Fishies

Five little fishies
Swimming in the pool,

The first one said,
"This pool is cool."

The second one said,
"This pool is deep."

The third one said,
"I'd like to sleep."

The fourth one said,
"Let's swim and dip."

The fifth one said,
"I see a ship."

The fisherman's line went
Splish, splish, splash,

(*fast*) And away the five
Little fishies dash!

33

Five Plump Peas

Even the babies love this simple little finger game. Act it out freely and with expression.

Five plump peas in a pea pod pressed,

And they grew...

One...grew...

Two...grew...

And they grew and

So did

ALL

never stopped...

the rest.

They grew SO fat that the pea...pod...

They grew...

POPPED!

Five Brown Buns

Lois learned this in Portland, Oregon, then got to use it in a Portuguese bakery in Toronto's Kensington Market while shooting *Sharon, Lois & Bram's Elephant Show*. It's the chant-of-choice whenever we step foot in a bakery — which is often!

Five brown **buns** in a **bak**ery **shop**,

Five brown **buns** with the **sugar** on the **top**;

Along came a **man** with a **penny** in his **hand**,

He took **one** bun…

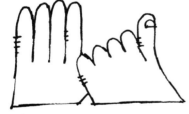

And **away** he **ran**.

Four brown **buns** in a **bakery shop**,
Four brown **buns** with the **sugar** on the **top**;
Along came a **man** with a **penny** in his **hand**,
He took **one** bun…
And **away** he **ran**.

Three brown **buns** in a **bak**ery **shop**… (*continue as in earlier verses*)

Two brown **buns** in a **bakery shop**…

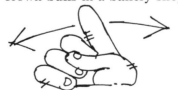

One brown **bun** in a **bakery shop**…

No brown **buns** in a **bakery shop**,
No brown **buns** with the **sugar** on the **top**;
Along came a **man** with a **penny** in his **hand**,
He took **one**…look…
(*fast*) And **away** he **ran**!

Little Peter Rabbit

This song tells a tiny perfect story with words and actions together. In concert, we stop singing the words a few at a time to an ever faster beat while continuing the actions, until all that's left are the gasps and giggles of a delighted audience.

March-like

① G ② ③ G7

Lit - tle Pe - ter Rab - bit had a flea up - on his ear.

REPEAT ABOVE ACTIONS TWICE MORE

① C ② G ③

Lit - tle Pe - ter Rab - bit had a flea up - on his ear.

① ② B7 ③ Em

Lit - tle Pe - ter Rab - bit had a flea up - on his ear and he

④ Am ⑤ D7 ⑥ G

flipped it and he flopped it and it flew a - way.

How to play:

When you sing this elimination song for the first time, sing all the words and do all the actions. The next time through, leave out the words in section 1 each time they appear in the song, but do the actions. The next time, leave out the words in sections 1 *and* 2, but continue doing the actions. Each time through, leave out another section of the words, continuing all the actions.

Arabella Miller

Once upon a time there was a little girl with an unusual pet...and a wonderful grandmother! (The tune here is *Twinkle, Twinkle, Little Star*.)

1. Lit - tle Ar - a - bel - la Mil - ler had a fuz - zy cat - er - pil - lar.

First it crawled up - on her moth - er, then up - on her ba - by broth - er.

(Verse 1 is spoken quickly; Verse 2 is sung)

They said, "Ar - a - bel - la Mil - ler! *Put a - way your cat - er - pil - lar!*"

2. Little Arabella Miller
   Had a fuzzy caterpillar.
   First it crawled upon her brother,
   Then upon her dear grandmother.
   Gran said, "Arabella Miller,
   How I love your caterpillar."

Think of this finger play as a story to act out with your voice and your face. Show how Arabella's family feels about that caterpillar. For the first verse, make a yucky face. For the second verse, a smiling one.

There Was a Little Man

Sharon and Lois learned this little finger play at Pinewoods Folk Music Camp, in Buzzards Bay, Massachusetts. It's a little-known treasure.

Act out this poem freely and with lots of expression. Say the last line as quickly as you can.

1.

There was a little man,

2.
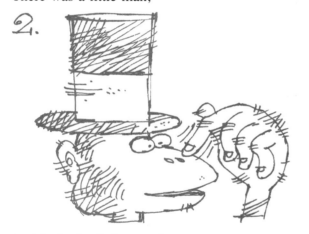
And he had a little crumb,

3.

And over the mountain he did run.

4.

With a belly full of fat,

5.

And a big tall hat…

6.

And a pancake stuck to his bum, bum, bum.

Cabin in the Wood

The object of this song is to eliminate the words, section by section, while remembering and doing the motions — so that eventually you have a tuneless, wordless song with a series of nonsense actions. Some practitioners of the art of "elimination singing" keep a steady pace throughout. Others speed up each time around until the pace is frantic. Tack on one last teeny-tiny go-round — and be sure to make the words and actions very quiet (shhhh!) and very, very tiny!

Flip-Flop, Wig-Wag
Action Songs

Body language is what an action song is all about. Sure, you can sing any of these songs with your hands folded in your lap and your legs neatly tucked underneath you. But what would Rags be without his flip-flop ears? How can you make peanut butter without digging up those peanuts? And there's no way to keep "one finger, one thumb" from moving. So just unfold those hands and untuck those feet, and get flopping!

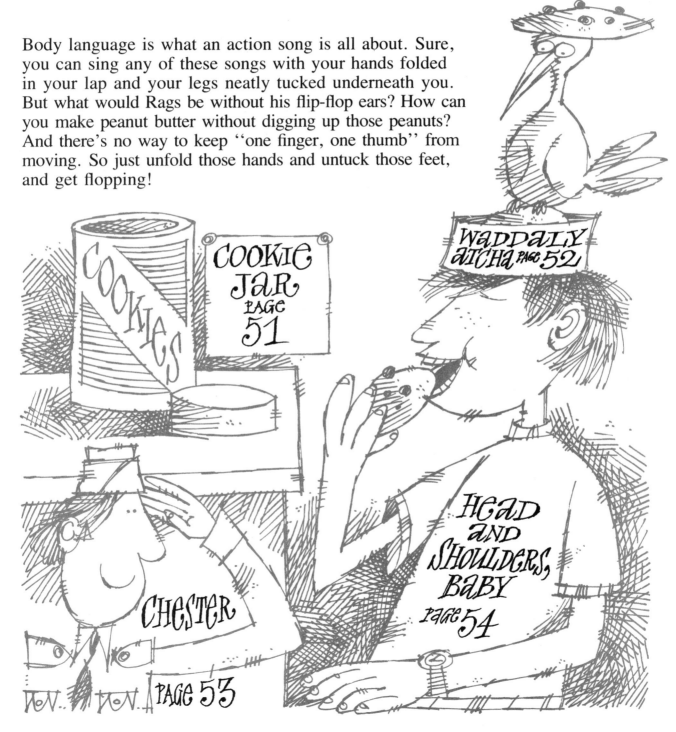

COOKIE JAR PAGE 51

WADDALY ATCHA PAGE 52

CHESTER PAGE 53

HEAD AND SHOULDERS, BABY PAGE 54

My Dog Rags

Everybody's favorite pal — my dog Rags.

Swingy

1. I have a dog and his name is Rags. He eats so much that his tum-my___ sags,___ His ears flip-flop and his tail wig-wags,___ and when he___ walks, he walks zig-zag.___ He goes flip-flop, wig-wag,

Chorus:

zig-zag.___ He goes flip-flop, wig-wag, zig-zag.___ He goes

flip flop

wig wag

zig zag

more flip-flops, wigs & wags

more zig-zags

more flip-flops, wig-wags & zig-zags

C   C7   F   A♭7   C   Gm   A7   D7 G7   C

flip - flop, wig - wag,   zig - zag,___   I   love___ Rags,___   and   he loves   me.

2. My dog Rags he loves to play.
   He rolls around in the mud all day.
   I whistle (*whistle*); he won't obey.
   He always runs the other way.

Rattlin' Bog

From England, a grand old sing-along, do-along song.

44

1. F   B♭   C7   F   B♭   F

1. Tree was in the bog,   and the bog down in the   val - ley - o.

2. - 9 F   B♭   F   B♭   C7

2. Branch was on the tree,   and the tree was on the bog,   and the bog down in the

F   B♭   F

val - ley - o.

Repeat the second ending for the rest of the verses, adding extra measures for extra words.

1. In that bog there was a tree…

2. On that tree there was a branch…

3. On that branch there was a twig…

4. On that twig there was a nest…

5. In that nest there was an egg…

6. In that egg there was a bird…

7. On that bird there was a feather…

8. On that feather there was a flea…

9. On that flea there was an elephant…

RATTLIN' BOG

One Finger, One Thumb

This is another one of those goofy camp songs that keeps you singing and moving in ever more complicated ways. Just do what the song says, and don't give up if you get confused. It takes time to do the song perfectly! And it's loads of fun when you don't!

Lively   **Cumulative round**

1. One fin - ger, one thumb, keep mov - ing, one fin - ger, one thumb, keep mov - ing, one fin - ger, one thumb, keep mov - ing, we'll all be mer - ry and bright._____ 2. One fin - ger, one thumb, one arm, keep mov - ing, one fin - ger, one thumb, one arm, keep mov - ing, one fin - ger, one thumb, one arm, keep mov - ing, we'll all be mer - ry and bright._____

3. One finger, one thumb, one arm, ONE LEG (*lift leg*)…

4. One finger, one thumb, one arm, one leg, A NOD OF THE HEAD (*nod head*)…

5. One finger, one thumb, one arm, one leg, a nod of the head, A SOUND OF THE PHTT (*make a raspberry sound*)…

6. One finger, one thumb, one arm, one leg, a nod of the head, a sound of the phtt, STAND UP, SIT DOWN…

How to play:

In the first verse, start with the pointer finger from one hand and the thumb from the other. Wiggle your finger and thumb when you sing each word. For the second verse, wiggle finger and thumb and add one arm (move elbow out and back). Keep adding parts of the body as mentioned (where the * appears in the music), getting faster with each verse until you reach a breakneck speed with the last verse.

If you're not totally exhausted, try it as a round! (Note the entry marks 1 and 2.) It is almost impossible to get to the end of the song without breaking up!

Pufferbellies

Moderately　　　　　　　　　　　　　　　　　　**2 - part round**

① Down　by　the sta - tion　ear - ly in　the morn - ing,

② See　the lit - tle puf - fer-bel - lies all　in　a　row,

See　the sta - tion-mas - ter　turn the lit - tle han - dle,

Puff,　puff! *Toot,　toot!* Off　we　go!

Peanut Butter

The granddaddy of all the peanut-butter-and-jelly songs, this one gets you moving and makes you hungry! And don't forget — peanuts are full of protein, and lots of good fiber if, like Elephant, you eat them with the shells on!

Emphasize the boldfaced words or syllables in this rhythmic chant.

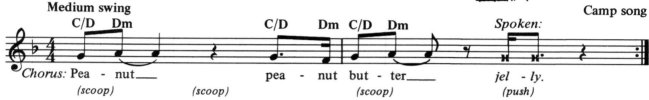

Medium swing

Camp song

Chorus: Pea - nut___ (scoop) (scoop) pea - nut but - ter___ (scoop) *Spoken:* jel - ly. (push)

1. **First** you dig the **pea**nuts (*dig with a shovel*)
   And you **dig** 'em, you **dig** 'em,
   you **dig** 'em, **dig** 'em, **dig** 'em.
   Then you **crush** 'em, you **crush** 'em, (*grind fist into palm*)
   You **crush** 'em, **crush** 'em, **crush** 'em.
   Then you **spread** 'em, you **spread** 'em, (*make spreading action with one hand on the other*)
   You **spread** 'em, **spread** 'em, **spread** 'em.
   Chorus

2. **Then** you pick the **ber**ries (*pick berries*)
   And you **pick** 'em, you **pick** 'em,
   You **pick** 'em, **pick** 'em, **pick** 'em.
   Then you **crush** 'em, you **crush** 'em, (*grind fist into palm*)
   You **crush** 'em, **crush** 'em, **crush** 'em.
   Then you **spread** 'em, you **spread** 'em, (*make spreading action*)
   You **spread** 'em, **spread** 'em, **spread** 'em.
   Chorus

3. **Then** you bite the **sand**wich (*take a bite out of a sandwich*)
   And you **bite** it, you **bite** it,
   You **bite** it, **bite** it, **bite** it.
   And you **munch** it, you **munch** it, (*exaggerate munching action as you speak*)
   You **munch** it, **munch** it, **munch** it.
   Then you **swal**low, you **swal**low, (*gulp!*)
   You **swal**low, **swal**low, **swal**low.
   Chorus

48

Back of a Crocodile

This sweet-sounding song tells a not-so-sweet story — but all in fun.

Action song

Oh, she sailed a - way on a sun - ny sum - mer day on the back of a croc - o - dile. "You see," said she, "he's as tame as he can be. I'll ride him down the Nile." The croc winked his eye as she waved them all good-bye wear - ing a hap - py smile. At the end of the ride the la - dy was in - side and the smile was on the croc - o - dile.

Did You Feed My Cow?

This is a robust call-and-answer chant with a good rhythmic beat and some expressive movement. It's all about cows and the special chores that farm folks do every day to look after them. The leader calls out the question, "Did you feed my cow?" and the group responds, "Yes, ma'am!"

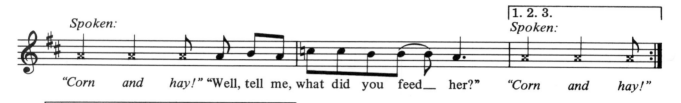

2. "Well, did you milk her real good?"　　"Yes, ma'am!"
   "Well, did you milk her like you should?"　　"Yes, ma'am!"
   "Well, show me, how did you milk her?"　　"Squish, squish, squish!"
   "Well, now, how did you milk her?"　　"Squish, squish, squish!"

3. "Well, did my cow get sick?"　　"Yes, ma'am!"
   "Oh, was she really, really sick?"　　"Yes, ma'am!"
   "Well, show me, how did she look?"　　"Uh, uh, uh!"
   "Again now, how did she look?"　　"Uh, uh, uh!"

4. "Well, did those buzzards come?"　　"Yes, ma'am!"
   "Oh, did those buzzards come?"　　"Yes, ma'am!"
   "Well, tell me, how did they come?"　　"Flop, flop, flop!"
   "Again now, how did they come?"　　"Flop, flop, flop!"
   "How did they come?"　　"Flop, flop, flop!"

To feel the beat when you sing "Yes, ma'am," keep your hands clapping and your feet walking in place.

Cookie Jar

A good way to get acquainted. Just sit in a circle and try to keep the name-game going with a steady beat. We've started the game with our own names; you start with yours.

Lively

Spoken:

Clapping chant

① ② ① ②

Zoom, zoom, zoom, my heart goes ka-boom, now who stole the cook-ie from the

cook-ie jar? Bram stole the cook-ie from the cook-ie jar. Who,

me? Yes, you! Could-n't be! Then who?

2. Lois stole the cookie from the cookie jar.
   Who, me?
   Yes, you!
   Couldn't be!
   Then who?

Last verse:

   Bram stole the cookie from the cookie jar.
   Who, me?
   Yes, you!
   Pos-si-bly!

How to play:
Hold hands with your neighbor on each side and swing your arms back and forth while you say, "Zoom, zoom, zoom, my heart goes kaboom." Then listen for your own name, answer at just the right time and call out another name until everyone has had a turn. Keep clapping and chanting to the beat all the while. Here's the clap pattern: Clap your own hands on 1; clap your neighbors' hands on 2. Repeat this pattern throughout the song.

Waddaly Atcha

Some songs seem like old friends from the very first singing. *Waddaly Atcha* is one of them.

"Doodle Doo Doo" by Art Kassel, Mel Stitzel and Ted Morse

Camp song

Chester

Here is a silly camp song in which the actions show that the song is not only about two guys but also about parts of the body. Can you find the words that have two meanings?

Lively

Camp song

Ches-ter, have you heard a-bout Har-ry? Just got back from the ar — my; I

hear he knows how to wear a rose, Hip, hip, hoo-ray for the ar — my.

You can sing this song two ways. Sing it only once through with the actions shown above, starting off slowly and getting faster and faster. Or, sing the song several times, getting faster each time the song is repeated. The faster you sing, the more confused you get!

WELCOME BACK HARRY!

HERO

Head and Shoulders, Baby

From the playground, a twosome game. Grab a partner, sing, clap, and get down, baby!

Moderate shuffle beat

1. Head and shoul-ders, ba - by; One, two, three. Head and shoul-ders, ba-by;

One, two, three. Head and shoul-ders, head and shoul-ders, head and shoul-ders, ba-by;

1. 2. 3. One, two, three.(2.Hips and thighs, ba-by;) 4. One, two, three.

Coda:

mf Ain't been to Fris - co,__ I ain't been to school,__ I ain't been to col-lege, but I'm

no-bod-y's fool.__ To the front, to the back, to the side, side, side.__ To the

2. Hips and thighs, baby...

3. Knees and ankles, baby...

4. Sing together, baby...

Make up additional verses and appropriate movements, such as:
"Throw the ball, baby... "
"Ride the pony, baby... "
"Do the twist, baby... "

Allons Jouer
Des Chansons en Français

Whether "Fait au Canada"—made in Canada—or adapted from the mother country, French-Canadian folk songs are a wonderfully special breed. They retain a kind of Gallic style, a combination of wit, charm and irony, that is at once uniquely French and yet perfectly accessible to an English-speaking audience. So enjoy this clutch of songs and dances and rhymes "à la mode de chez nous"—as we do at our place!

AH SI MON MOINE

SAVEZ-VOUS PLANTER LES CHOUX? PAGE 68

PAGE 66

La BASTRINGUE PAGE 67

Monté sur un éléphant

This is a charming song about climbing on one, two…ten…a thousand elephants! It's high — and it's scary!

Moderately

Quebec

1. Mon -té sur un él - é -phant,_____ c'est haut,_____ c'est haut._____ Mon -té sur un él - é -phant,_____ c'est haut, c'est ef - fray - ant._____ Mon - cile._____

last time ritard.

1. 2. 3.

4.

2. Monté sur deux éléphants…

3. Monté sur dix éléphants…

4. Monté sur mille éléphants…

un crocodile

c'est bas

c'est imbécile

5. Monté sur un crocodile,
   C'est bas, c'est bas.
   Monté sur un crocodile,
   C'est bas, c'est imbécile.

Translation:
1. Climbing on an elephant's back,
   It's high and it's scary.

2. Climbing on two elephants' backs…

3. Climbing on ten elephants' backs…

4. Climbing on a thousand elephants' backs…

5. Climbing on a crocodile's back,
   It's low and you gotta be crazy to do it.

Sur le pont d'Avignon

Surely one of the most beloved and well-known French singing games.

Lively

Singing game

① Chorus:

Sur le pont d'Av - ign - on, on y dan - se, on y dan - se.

② Sur le pont d'Av - ign - on, on y dan - se, tous en ronde. *Fine*

Translation:

Chorus:

On the bridge of Avignon,
Everyone is dancing.
On the bridge of Avignon,
Everyone is dancing in a circle.

Actions:

During part 1 of the chorus, everyone holds hands in a circle and skips around to the left. Reverse the direction of the circle movement in part 2.

1. Les jeunes filles
2. Les pou-pées } font comme ci.
3. Les gren-ouilles

Les gar-çons
Les sol-dats } font comme ça.
Les gor-illes

1. The young girls go like this,
   The boys go like that.

Girls step to the center of the circle, curtsy and return to their places. Then the boys go to the center, bow and return.

Chorus

Repeat chorus actions.

2. The dolls go like this,
   The soldiers go like that.

All move to the center and back like stiff walking dolls. Then march to the center like soldiers, salute and return.

Chorus

Repeat chorus actions.

3. The frogs go like this,
   The gorillas go like that.

Hop like frogs to the center and back, then thump your chests like gorillas, in and back.

Chorus

Repeat chorus actions.

If you speak French, or are learning to, make up some of your own verses using other characters or animals.

Jamais on n'a vu

This is a French round *très tendre*. The words mean "You've never seen, nor will you ever see, a tiny mouse in a cat's ear."

Slowly and sweetly

① Cmaj7/9 Fmaj7 ② 4 - part round

Ja - mais on n'a vu, vu, vu,_____ Ja - mais on n'ver -

Em7 Edim ③ Dm7

ra - ra - ra,_____ Une pe - tite sou - ris - ris - ris_____

④ G9 Cmaj7 C6

_____ dans l'o - reille d'un chat, chat, chat._____

Michaud

This is a delightful song that tells about what happened when young Michaud climbed an apple tree. The song can be sung in French, in English or bilingually, in unison or in call-and-response style.

Traditional, English translation by Alan Mills
Quebec

Brightly

Mi - chaud est mon - té dans un beau pom - mier, Mi - chaud est mon - té dans un
Mi - chaud climbed u - up an ap - ple tree, Mi - chaud climbed u - up an

beau pom - mier. La branche a cas - sé, Mi - chaud est tom - bé, où
ap - ple tree. The bra - anch it broke. Snapped with a crack. Oh,

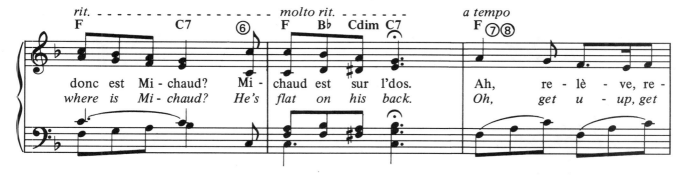

rit. _____ *molto rit.* _____ *a tempo*

donc est Mi - chaud? Mi - chaud est sur l'dos. Ah, re - lè - ve, re -
where is Mi - chaud? He's flat on his back. Oh, get u - up, get

lè - ve, re - lè - ve, ah, re - lè - ve, re - | lè - ve, Mi - chaud. | lè - ve, Mi - chaud.
u - up, get u - up. Oh, get u - up, get | u - up, Mi - chaud. | u - up, Mi - chaud.

rall. _____

For a bilingual version, sing line 1 in French, line 2 in English, line 3 in French, and so on. The English version is not so much an exact translation as an English adaptation.

For example, "Michaud est tombé" means "Michaud fell down," not "snapped with a crack."

Fais do do

This lullaby is as well known in the French-speaking world as *Rock-a-Bye Baby* is in the English. "Fais do do" is French for "Baby, go to sleep." In this song, the baby is being sung to sleep by an older brother or sister.

Gently

Quebec lullaby

Fais do - do, Co - las mon p'tit frè - re fais do -

do, t'au - ras du lo - lo. Ma - man est en haut, elle

64

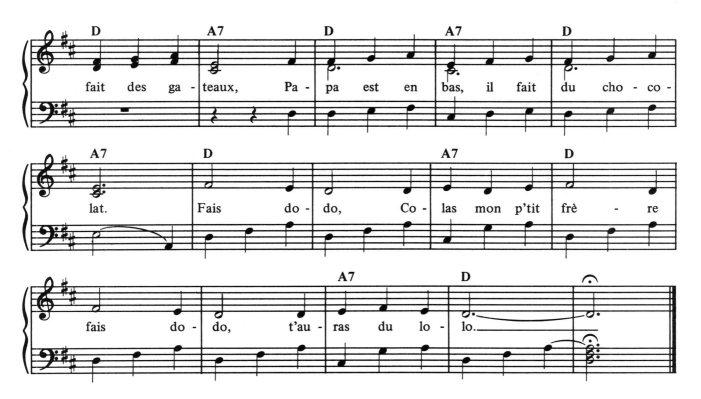

Translation:

Go to sleep, Colas, my little brother,
Go to sleep and you'll have a treat.
Mama is upstairs making cakes;
Papa is downstairs making chocolate.
Go to sleep, Colas, my little brother,
Go to sleep and you'll have a treat.

In some versions the baby's name is Colin.
Use any name you like.

Ah si mon moine

This popular folk song from Quebec, full of wonderful "dancey" rhymes, revolves around a comical play on words. In French, "moine" has two meanings: a spinning top and a monk in religious orders.

Brightly

Quebec dance tune

1. Ah si mon moi - ne vou - lait dan - ser, ah si mon moi - ne vou - lait dan - ser, un

ca - pu - chon je lui don - ne - rais, un ca - pu - chon je lui don - ne - rais.

Chorus:

Dan - se mon moine dan - se, tu n'en - tends pas la dan - se, tu

n'en - tends pas mon mou - lin - lon - lin, tu n'en - tends pas mon mou - lin mar - cher.

2. … un ceinturon je lui donnerais.
   Chorus

3. … un beau psautier je lui donnerais.
   Chorus

4. S'il n'avait fait veux di pauvreté,
   Bien d'autres choses je lui donnerais.
   Chorus

Translation:

1. Oh, if my monk (top) would dance with me
   I would give him a new cow!

Ch: Dance, my monk, dance!
   You don't hear the dance,
   You don't hear my mill,
   You don't hear my mill working.

2. … I'd give him a new sash!

3. … I'd give him a fine psalm book!

4. If he had not taken his vows of poverty,
   Many other things would I have given him.

La Bastringue

La Bastringue is an old courtly dance from France that came to the New World and got "Quebec-ified." The song tells the story of an older gent who gallantly persuades a pretty young girl to dance the "Bastringue" with him. Despite his valiant efforts to keep up with her, however, he is finally done in by the corns on his feet! Two groups or individuals should sing this as a dialogue.

Brightly

Quebec dance tune

Ma - de-moi-selle, vou-lez-vous dan - ser la bas-trin - gue, la bas - trin - gue?

Ma - de-moi-selle, vou-lez-vous dan - ser, La bas-tringue va com - men - cer.

Oui, mon - sieur, je veut bien dan - ser la bas - trin - gue, la bas - trin - gue.

Oui, mon - sieur, je veut bien dan - ser, c'est pour vous ac - com - pa - gner.

2. Mademoiselle, vous avez dansé
   La Bastringue, la Bastringue.
   Mademoiselle, vous avez dansé,
   Vous allez vous fatiguer.

   Ah, non, monsieur, je sais bien danser
   La Bastringue, la Bastringue.
   Ah, non, monsieur, je sais bien danser,
   Je suis prête à recommencer.

3. Mademoiselle, je peut plus danser
   La Bastringue, la Bastringue.
   Mademoiselle, je peut plus danser
   Parce que j'ai des cors au pieds!

Translation:
1. Miss, would you like to dance
        la Bastringue with me?
    It's about to start.
    Yes, sir, I'd be very happy to
        accompany you in la Bastringue.

2. Miss, you've been dancing la Bastringue
        for a while now,
    And I'm afraid you'll get tired.
    Oh, no, sir, I'm good at this dance
    And I'm ready to start again.

3. Miss, I can't go on with this dance
    Because I have corns on my feet!

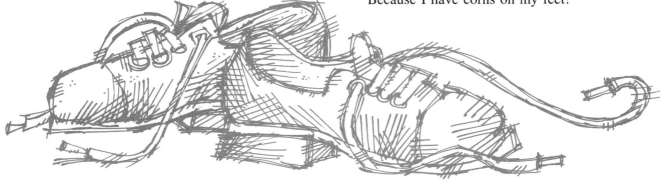

Savez-vous planter les choux?

"Do you know how to plant cabbages," asks this classic French children's song, "the way we do at home?" Of course! — with our hands, our feet and even our cheeks!

Accompany the second part of each verse with the appropriate body action or sound.

Jig - with a bounce

French

Sa - vez - vous plan - ter les choux, à la mo - de, à la

mo - de, Sa - vez - vous plan - ter les choux, à la mo - de de chez

nous? On les plante a - vec les mains, à la mo - de, à la

mo - de, On les plante a - vec les mains, à la mo - de de chez

1. nous. 2. nous, à la mo - de de chez nous!

68

2. On les plante avec les mains, à la mode, à la mode,
   On les plante avec les mains, à la mode, de chez nous.

3. On les plante avec les doigts…

4. On les plante avec les joues…

5. On les plante avec la langue…

6. On les plante avec les levres…

7. On les plante en riant…

Translation:
Do you know how to plant cabbages,
As we do, as we do,
Do you know how to plant cabbages,
As we do at our place.
We plant them with our hands…
(*fingers, cheeks, tongue, lips, laughing*)

And That's No Joke!
Silly Songs and Rhymes

Music and humor combine to create some of the best fun possible—ridiculous rhymes, raucous rounds, kooky camp songs and wacky walks.

We played "Schlemiel Schlemazel" with the children of Yampupata, a remote village on the shores of Lake Titicaca in Bolivia. There we discovered once again that children everywhere love a silly song and a good giggle.

ONCE I SAW THREE GOATS
PAGE 77

THE ANTS GO MARCHING
PAGE 78

MICHAEL FINNEGAN
PAGE 79

I AM SLOWLY GOING CRAZY

PAGE 79

Tall Silk Hat

An old-time favorite in summer camp, on the school bus or even on the subway. Take the familiar Italian tune *Funiculi, Funicula*, add some zany lyrics and you've got a new classic.

Brightly

Camp song

One day____ as I was rid-ing on the sub-way,____ my tall silk hat,____ my tall silk hat.____ I laid____ it down up-on the seat be-side me,____ my tall silk hat,____ my tall silk hat.____ A great____ big la-dy came and sat up-on it,____ my tall silk hat,____ it went like that!____ A great____ big la-dy came and sat up-on it,____ my tall silk hat,____ it went like that!____ Chris-to-pher Co-lum-bus, now wad-da ya think of that?____ A great big la-dy sat up-on my hat. My hat she broke and that's no joke, my hat she broke and that's no joke! Chris-to-pher Co-lum-bus, now wad-da ya think of that? *HEY!*

72

Here are two wacky walks to use on the way
to school, to camp, to work, to play…or
just as you walk the dog.

Schlemiel, Schlemazel

1,2,3,4,5,6,7,8,9,10
Schlemiel
Schlemazel
A-hasenpfeffer
Hootchy, Kootchy

1,2,3,4,5,6,7,8,9,10
(start with right foot and walk forward 10 steps)

SCHLEMIEL, SCHLEMAZEL
(right foot out)   (left foot out)

A-HASEN   PFEFFER
(bend down)   (stand up)

HOOTCHY, KOOTCHY
(bump hips…one side, then other)

Left, Left

Chant this rhyme while you walk.

L R   L R
Left…left…

L   R   L R
I **had** a good job that I **left**,

L   R   L R   L
And **do** you think it was **RIGHT**,

R   L   R L   R
To **leave** the job that I **LEFT**?

The walk:
Everyone marches forward, left foot first,
four steps per line. On "was RIGHT,"
take two quick steps (left, right) so that the
right foot is now out front. And on the last "I
LEFT," take two more quick steps (right,
left) so that the left foot leads again.

73

Little Tommy Tinker

We love to sing this song in concert and watch the audience jump up, throwing their arms in the air at different times. Frequently it turns into hilarious confusion, and then we three have the best seats in the house!

Lightly   ① ②   4 - or 8 - part round

Lit - tle Tom-my Tin - ker   sat up-on   a   clin - ker   and   he   be - gan   to

Throw arms up   ③   ④

cry: "Oh, Ma,_____   oh, Ma,"_____   poor lit - tle in - no-cent guy!

I Sat Next to the Duchess at Tea

The next time your stomach rumbles at the wrong time, think of the poor Duchess.

Moderately   ①   ②   4 - part round

I   sat   next   to   the   duch-ess   at   tea.___   It   was   just   as   I

③

thought   it   would   be.___   Her   rum - bl - ings   ab - dom - in - al   were

④

sim - ply quite phe - nom-en - al   and   ev - ery - one thought it was   me!

John Jacob Jingleheimer Schmidt

Each time you sing this song, get softer and softer — except for the "tra-la-la," which gets louder and louder. Last time through, the words are just mouthed silently, but the final "John Jacob Jingleheimer Schmidt" is shouted as loudly as possible.

Lively

Camp song

John Ja - cob Jin - gle -heim - er Schmidt, that's my name, too.___

_____ When -ev - er I go out, the peo -ple al -ways shout, "There goes

John Ja - cob Jin - gle -heim - er Schmidt," tra la la la la la la...

Ticka-Tacka

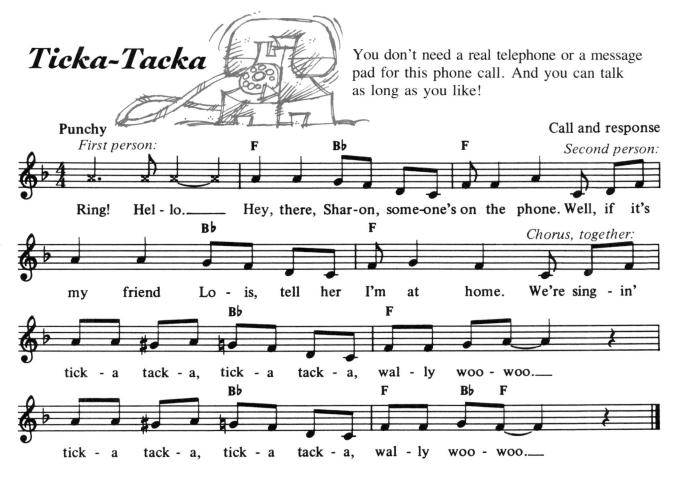

You don't need a real telephone or a message pad for this phone call. And you can talk as long as you like!

Punchy

Call and response

First person:

Second person:

Ring! Hel - lo.___ Hey, there, Shar-on, some-one's on the phone. Well, if it's

my friend Lo - is, tell her I'm at home. We're sing - in'

Chorus, together:

tick - a tack -a, tick - a tack -a, wal - ly woo - woo.___

tick - a tack -a, tick - a tack -a, wal - ly woo - woo.___

Vista

All of our kids have at one time or another taught us different versions of this old camp song. Here are two of our favorites.

Moderately   *Echo:*   Echo chant

Flea!   *Flea!*   Flea, fly!   *Flea, fly!*   Flea, fly, flo.

Flea, fly, flo.   Vis - ta.   *Vis - ta.*   Ma - ma la - ma cu - ma la - ma

cu - ma la vis - ta.____ Oh, no, no, no,____ not da vis - ta.

Es - sa mee - ny sol - la mee - ny oo - wal - la wal - la mee - ny

Es - sa mee - ny sol - la mee - ny oo - wal - la wah.

Eesch bil - ly ah - ten dot - ten, bo - bo be dee - ten dot - ten, tshsh...........

Try it this way, too.

Flea (*Flea!*)
Flea fly (*Flea fly!*)
Flea fly mosquito (*Flea fly mosquito!*)
Oh no-no no more mosquitoes (*Oh no-no no more mosquitoes*),
Itchy-itchy, scratchy-scratchy, ooh I got one down my backy (*Itchy-itchy, scratchy-scratchy, ooh I got one down my backy*),
Chase that big bad bug, make him go away (*Chase that big bad bug, make him go away*),
Shoo!

Once I Saw Three Goats

We often sing this goofy rhyming song in teacher workshops and have gathered some neat rhymes that we pass on to you for inspiration.

Brightly

Rhyming song

Once I saw three goats and they were wear-ing coats, tra-la -la-la-la -la-la-la fun-ny lit-tle goats. And then I saw three cats, and they were wear-ing hats, tra-la -la-la -la -la-la-la fun-ny lit-tle cats.

Some other rhymes:
pigs — wigs
kittens — mittens
doves — gloves
flies — ties
bees — skis
eels — high heels
gophers — loafers
lambies — jammies
bear — taking off his underwear
elephant — talking on the telephant!
Had enough?

Now, how about drawing some of these clothes-wearing animals?

The Ants Go Marching

This is our version of a number-rhyming song most youngsters seem to know. The made-up verses should be as silly as the subject matter itself.

Moderately

Rhyming chant

Spoken:

The ants are coming!

1. The ants go march-ing one by one, hoo-rah;____ hoo-rah,____ The ants go march-ing one by one, hoo-rah,____ hoo-rah;____ The ants go march-ing one by one, the lit-tle one stopped to have some fun, *Chorus:* And they all go march-ing 'round and a-round, and down in the ground, and up the drain, and out in the rain.

2. The ants go marching two by two, hoorah, hoorah; *(repeat)*
   The ants go marching two by two, the little one stopped to say Achoo!
   Chorus

3. The ants go marching three by three, hoorah, hoorah; *(repeat)*
   The ants go marching three by three, they looked as silly as can be!
   Chorus

Make up your own verses, but try to avoid the cliché number-rhymes that seem to come up so often (like ''shoe'' with ''two'' and ''tree'' with ''three'').

I Am Slowly Going Crazy

Kids want to sing this song anytime; grown-ups *need* to sing it at the end of a long day!

Action song

Moderately

I am slow - ly go - ing cra - zy, one two three four five six switch.

Cra - zy go - ing slow - ly am I, six five four three two one switch.

Divide into three groups. Group 1 sings the song very slowly, as written. Group 2 starts the second time around by singing it twice as fast so that they get through it twice for the first group's once. The third group joins the third time around, singing four times as fast. This last speed is very hard to sing — tapping the beat helps keep everyone together. Sometimes!

Michael Finnegan

Repeat faster and faster each time through.

Brightly

Camp song

I know a man named Mi - chael Fin - ne - gan, He has whis - kers on his chin a - gain, shaved them off, but they grew in a - gain, poor old Mi - chael Fin - ne - gan, be - gin a - gain:

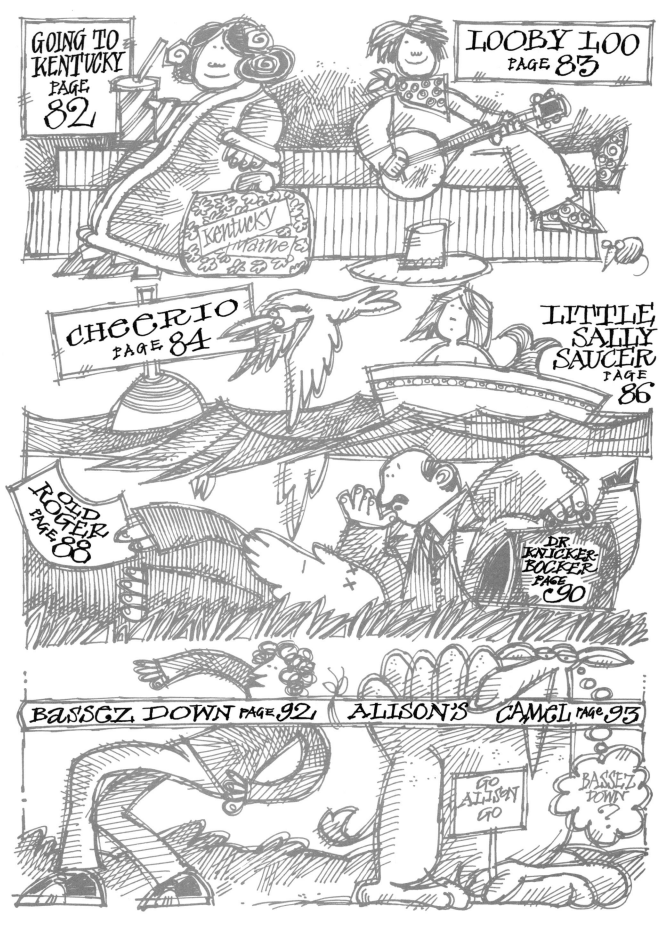

Shake It, Baby
Singing Games

You can play these games anywhere, but they seem to work best outside, where the space is big and the mood easy, and the players can let go and have a good time. Once they've mastered the song and the basic form, the energy of the game takes over and the fun begins. Each player urges the next to join in, to keep things moving, to try something new. And when the game really gets going, it's hard to stop. These games ought to keep you going for a long time.

PUNCHINELLO 47 PAGE 94

CHARLIE OVER THE OCEAN PAGE 95

DOWN IN THE VALLEY TWO BY TWO PAGE 97

THE MUFFIN MAN PAGE 98

PAWPAW PATCH PAGE 96

Going to Kentucky

When we sing this in concert, it's great fun to watch all the youngsters and grown-ups together "shake it like a milkshake!"

Brightly

Playground game

① We're go-ing to Ken-tuck-y, we're go-ing to the fair, to see a se-ño-ri-ta with ros-es in her hair, so ② shake it, ba-by, shake it, shake it if you can, so ③ shake it like a milk-shake, and drink it if you can, so rum-ble to the bot-tom, rum-ble to the top, ④ turn a-round and turn a-round un-til you make a stop!

How to play:

Find the numbers 1, 2, 3 and 4 in the song and learn the actions that go with each part.

Part 1 — Players form a circle, with one player in the middle. All sing and clap while the middle player walks around, pretending to be a señorita with roses in her hair.

Part 2 — The señorita shakes any part of her body, or her whole body, while players copy her.

Part 3 — All players rumble to the bottom by doing the twist, gradually getting closer to the ground. Then they rumble to the top by twisting higher and higher.

Part 4 — The señorita closes her eyes and extends one hand with a finger pointed, turning around and around. Whoever she is pointing to at the end of the song is the new señorita.

Looby Loo

Some folks believe this traditional play party refers back to the Saturday night family bath in a galvanized bucket. The first one in got the boiling water right from the stove — so hot that when you put your "right foot in" you immediately took your "right foot out" lest you scald your toes. We call our version of this old game *The Saturday Night Bath Blues*.

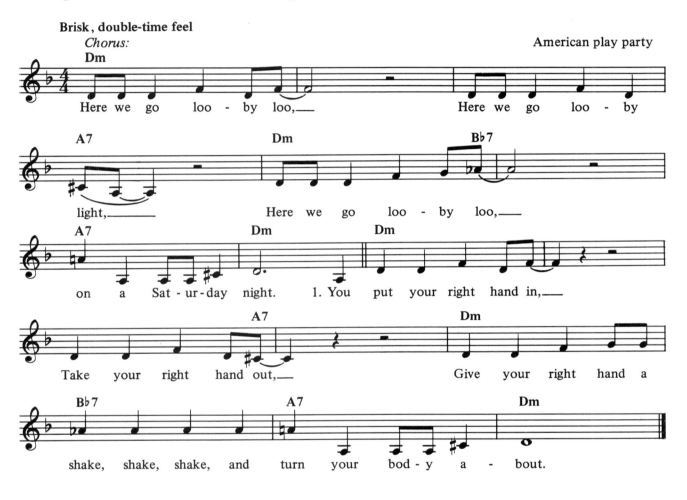

Brisk, double-time feel

Chorus:

American play party

Here we go loo - by loo,__ Here we go loo - by light,__ Here we go loo - by loo,__ on a Sat - ur - day night. 1. You put your right hand in,__ Take your right hand out,__ Give your right hand a shake, shake, shake, and turn your bod - y a - bout.

2. You put your left foot in...
   Chorus

3. You put your right hip in...
   Chorus

4. You put your whole self in...
   Chorus

You can play this game alone, in pairs or in a circle. Just dance to the chorus and make up your own verses as you go along. You could try "big toe," "right ear," "mustache" or "beard."

Cheerio

This playground game, learned from some schoolchildren in Flint, Michigan, is a prime example of an adult affliction we call ''playground fever.'' It's a seasonal affliction that comes upon us in the spring and summer when the children in the streets and playgrounds put away their snowsuits and boots and take out balls and skipping ropes and begin the familiar ritual of skipping, chanting, singing and clapping. It begins by watching and listening, and if you look interested and eager, it will often lead to a shy invitation to join in. Then the fever reaches its peak, for if you've the stamina to stay with it, there are new claps to master and rhymes to remember and even dance steps to work out. And then, inevitably, comes the sweet moment when the rhyme is familiar, is remembered exactly, word for word, unchanged, unaltered through time and generations of children. For that brief moment, the barriers of age and experience fall away, and you are once again a child among children. We hope *Cheerio* helps you remember the rhymes of your childhood. You can ''ooo-ah'' for as few or as many parts of your body as you wish.

Bluesy   Playground game

① Bb   Eb7   Bb   Eb7

Here we go cheer - i - o, cheer - i - o, cheer - i - o,

Bb   Eb7   1. F7   Bb   2. F7   Bb   F7

here we go cheer - i - o all night_ long._ all night_ long._ Oh, well, I

② Bb   Eb7   Bb   Eb7   Bb Cm Dm Eb

looked a-round the cor - ner _ and what did I see?_ I saw a great big man from

C7 F7 Bb F7   Bb   Eb7   Bb   Eb7

Cal - gar - y _
(*or* Ten - nes - see)_ Oh, well, I bet - cha five dol - lars I can knock 'em_ flat,_ when I

shake my skirts a - bove my_ knees._ Yes, I can knock 'em flat in

Cal - gar - y_
(or Ten - nes - see)_ Oh, well, my ma - ma called the doc - tor,_ the doc - tor said,_ I got a

pain in my stom - ach, ooo - ah,_ I got a pain in my el - bow,

ooo - ah._ Roll - a, roll - a, roll - a, pinch, roll - a, roll - a, roll - a, pinch,

1.
oom che wah - wah, oom che wah - wah,

2.
and that's all!

HERE WE GO   CHEERIO, CHEERIO

Little Sally Saucer

We all remember the sweet Miss Sally Saucer from our nursery days. But how about a disco Sally? Try this version just for fun — and "shake it, baby, shake it."

Shake it to the ver - y one that | you love the best!

Bb/C
Whisper:

Shake it, *shake it!*

C9

2. Little Sammy Saucer… (*etc.*)
   Shake it in a pot, *Shake it, shake it!*
   Shake it in a pan, *Shake it, shake it!*
   Shake it like a milkshake and drink it if you
   can! (*etc.*)

How to play:

Form a circle, with Sally sitting in the middle. During part 1, Sally pretends to cry. She slowly rises during part 2, and in part 3 she shakes whatever part of her body she chooses (arms, hips, shoulders…) over to the one she "loves the best." Repeat until everyone has had a turn to be Sally or Sammy, and make sure everyone in the circle "shakes" along.

Old Roger

The littles especially love acting out this traditional English singing game about old Roger and his apple tree.

Moderately bright

England

1. Old Ro-ger is dead and he lies in his grave, lies in his grave, lies in his grave. Old Ro-ger is dead and he lies in his grave, E, I, lies in his grave.

1. Old Roger is dead and he lies in his grave...

2. They planted an apple tree over his head...

3. The apples grew ripe and they all fell off...
   (*Six apples hold on to the branches, three to a branch. As the players sing this verse, the apples fall to the ground, one at a time.*)

How to play:

The players make a circle. A leader chooses the players to be Roger, the tree, six apples and the old woman, and each verse is sung after the players are in place inside the circle.

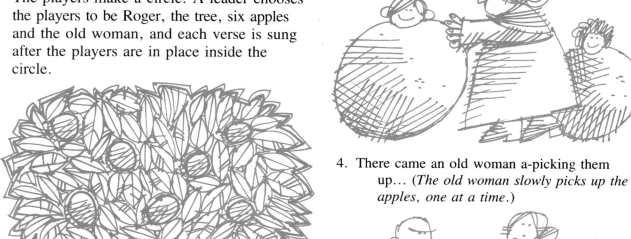

4. There came an old woman a-picking them up... (*The old woman slowly picks up the apples, one at a time.*)

5. Old Roger got up and gave her a knock... (*Old Roger gets up and pretends to knock the old woman with an imaginary stick.*)

6. (*faster*) Which made the old woman go clippity-clap... (*The old woman runs around the circle with Roger in hot pursuit.*)

Dr. Knickerbocker

Another favorite call-and-response playground game. Sometimes the players add more rhymes just to keep the game going.

let's get— the rhy - thm of the hips *(whoo-wee!).* Now, we got— the rhy - thm of the

hips, *(whoo-wee!).* 5. Now, let's get— the rhy - thm of the num - ber— nine!

One, two, three, four, five, six, sev - en, eight, nine!_____

How to play:

The players make a circle, with one person in the middle. All sing and clap together as shown in the illustrations. Keep up this together-out clap pattern all through the song. Always clap together on ''Now'' and out on ''let's'' and ''we.''

During ''the rhythm of the number nine!'', the leader walks around, tapping a different player for each number, while all count loudly to nine. Number nine then joins the leader in the middle and they clap together and start all over. If you play until everyone is chosen, you'll have a new circle that looks just like the old one!

Make up your own verses, such as:
''sneeze'' *(show a sneeze)*
''knees'' *(knock knees together)*
''chest'' *(pound chest like Tarzan)*

Bassez Down

This singing game is a variant of the popular limbo dance.

West Indian singing game

With a lively Caribbean beat

mf Bas - sez, Ma - ma, Bas - sez down, Bas-sez in the morn-ing,

Bas-sez down. Ba - | Bas-sez down. 1. Bas-sez down, Mis-sie Mar-y,

Bas-sez down, Bas-sez down, Mis-sie Mar-y, Bas-sez down, Bas-sez

down, Mis-sie Mar-y, Bas-sez down, Bas-sez in the morn - ing, Bas-sez down.

How to play:

The players start in a circle, with a girl in the middle. Everyone sings and moves to the rhythm of the chorus. On "Bassez down, Missie Mary," the girl in the middle starts to move slowly down toward the floor, any way she wishes as long as she keeps moving to the music. The players copy her. On the last "down," everyone sits flat on the floor. The girl in the middle chooses a new leader (a boy, to be Miste' Billy), while everyone stands and sings the chorus.

There are many different ways to move your body slowly down to the floor. It takes patience and control!

Alison's Camel

We learned this circle game from some Grade 3 Brownies, who kindly demonstrated and then wrote out the whole song, each and every word, about five pages in all. We still have those original lyrics, which we treasure.

Lively   Playground game

1. Al-i-son's cam-el has ten humps, Al-i-son's cam-el has ten humps,

Al-i-son's cam-el has ten humps, So go, Al-i-son, go—boom boom boom!

no humps, *so Al-i-son has A HORSE, of course!*

How to play:

This song is sung standing fairly close together in a circle. Each verse is a little faster than the one before until, by the last verse, the song is clipping along.

Sing all the way down from ten humps to:

Alison's camel has no humps,
Alison's camel has no humps,
Alison's camel has no humps,
(*very slowly*) So Alison has a HORSE, of course!

Punchinello 47

Punchinello was a character of old Italian theater (commedia dell'arte). He was a sly, comic servant with a hook nose and a humpback, always getting into trouble and cleverly avoiding punishment. What can *you* do, Punchinello?

Bright   Playground game

One, two, three, four! Look who's com-in' through the door!

1. Look who is here, Pun-chi-nel-lo for-ty-sev-en, Look who is here, Pun-chi-nel-lo for-ty-eight. 2. What can you do, Pun-chi-nel-lo for-ty sev-en, What can you do, Pun-chi-nel-lo for-ty-eight? 3. We can do it, too, Pun-chi-nel-lo for-ty-sev-en, We can do it, too, Pun-chi-nel-lo for-ty-eight. *Great!*

4. Who do you choose, Punchinello 47,
   Who do you choose, Punchinello 48?

How to play:
Make a circle, with one player in the middle. Here are the actions:

In verse 1: The players sing and clap while Punchinello skips around inside the circle.

In verse 2: Punchinello stands in the center and makes a motion — using hands, feet, body or a combination of all three in any way he or she chooses. The players clap and sing.

In verse 3: Punchinello continues his motion, but now the players copy his motion. ("We can do it, too...")

In verse 4: Punchinello closes his or her eyes; with arm stretched out and finger pointing he slowly turns while the players clap and sing. He stops when the verse ends, opens his eyes and walks straight toward the player he is pointing to...the new Punchinello.

Note: Make sure everyone claps strongly and moves with the beat. When playing this game for the first time, the children can copycat the leader's movements; then a child can take over as leader. After that, everyone should try not to copy the motion of the Punchinello before him or her. To help the children loosen up (and develop new ideas for movement), have them listen and move to records with different beats and styles (march music, Latin, disco, etc.). All of this will help the children respond to the music in a more free and unselfconscious manner.

Charlie Over the Ocean

Gather a whole gang together outside, make a circle and choose a Charlie to run like the wind. Charlie sings each line of the song first and the group echoes him.

Moderately

Echo chant

Charlie: Char - lie o - ver the o - cean. Group: (Char - lie o - ver the o - cean.)

Char - lie o - ver the sea. (Char - lie o - ver the sea.)

Char - lie caught a black - bird. (Char - lie caught a black - bird.)

Can't catch me! (Can't catch me!)

Can't catch me!

How to play:

Charlie sings and skips around the outside of the circle. As the group echoes the last word, Charlie taps the shoulder of the closest person, who runs after Charlie, trying to tag him before Charlie gets back to that person's space. If Charlie gets tagged, he's "it" again; if he gets home safely, the new person is Charlie.

You can *chase* Charlie or *race* Charlie. *Chase* means you run after him. *Race* means you run the opposite way from Charlie to see who can get back to the empty space first. Mind your heads when you race!

Pawpaw Patch

The pawpaw is the fruit of the pawpaw tree, found in the southern United States and as far north as Kansas and Michigan. It looks like a thick, short banana with greenish-brown skin, but it doesn't taste very good. This play-party game, named for the fruit, was enjoyed by folks back in pioneer days and is still popular today.

1. Where, oh, where is sweet lit-tle Nel-lie? Where, oh, where is sweet lit-tle Nel-lie? Where, oh, where is sweet lit-tle Nel-lie? Way down yon-der in the paw-paw patch! Come on, boys, let's go find her, Come on, boys, let's go find her, Come on, boys, let's go find her, Way down yon-der in the paw-paw patch!

Chorus:

Pick-in' up the paw-paws, put 'em in your pock-et, Pick-in' up the paw-paws, put 'em in your pock-et, Pick-in' up the paw-paws, put 'em in your pock-et, Way down yon-der in the paw-paw patch!

How to play:

During the verse: Players sit at random. The child who is "it" hides while the other players close their eyes. When Nellie or Billy is hidden, the children sing this verse, with eyes open. Then either all the boys or all the girls, or one boy or one girl, set out to look for the hidden child. Keep singing this verse until the child is found.

During the chorus: Everybody who has been out hunting bends down and scoops up pretend pawpaws, together with the child who has been found. Then the game starts all over with a new "it."

Down in the Valley Two by Two

This slave game, well over 100 years old, came to us by way of the wonderful Mrs. Bessie Jones of the Georgia Sea Islands. She learned this game from her grandfather, who explained it this way: when you're "down" and feeling blue, you've got to try to make yourself "rise" and feel good. And when you do, it's good to help your friends rise and feel happy with you, "two by two."

Moderately

Southern U.S.

2. Let me see you make another motion...

3. Let me see you make a monkey motion...

The Muffin Man

It wasn't so long ago in England that the muffin man could be seen coming down the road each Sunday, ringing his bell and carrying a load of fresh muffins on a board balanced on his head. The muffins were neatly covered by a clean cloth. In England, muffins are not as we know them (sweet round cakes baked in fluted paper liners); they are what we call crumpets.

Brightly and lightly

England

mf 1. Oh, do you know the Muf-fin Man, the Muf-fin Man, the Muf-fin Man? Oh, do you know the Muf-fin Man who lives in Dru-ry Lane? Oh, Lane?

2. Yes, I know…

3. Two (four, eight…all) of us know…

How to play:
Form a circle, with one person in the middle. In verse 1, the person in the middle walks around and then faces someone in the circle and sings, ''Do you know the Muffin Man,'' while doing the Muffin Man step. In verse 2, that person answers, ''Yes, I know the Muffin Man,'' while doing the same

step. In verse 3, the two players hold hands and skip around inside the circle. Both people in the middle start the game again at verse 1 by singing to two new people. The number of people who "know the Muffin Man" doubles until four, eight...all know him and there is no more circle.

The Muffin Man Step:
Hold your arms crossed against your chest and jump up, putting your right heel forward on the ground. Then jump up again with your left heel forward.

Choosing Rhymes

If you're tired of "Eeny Meeny Miney Mo," here are some other delightful choosing rhymes.

Eeny Meeny My
Eeny meeny my,
Po-pa tisha pie.
Isha-misha,
Po-pa-tisha,
Eeny meeny my.

Bee, Bee, Bumblebee
Bee, bee, bumblebee,
Sting a man upon his knee.
Sting a pig upon his snout —
I declare that you are OUT!

One Potato, Two Potato
One potato, two potato,
Three potato, four,
Five potato, six potato,
Seven potato, more.

Inky Pinky Ponky
Inky pinky ponky,
Daddy bought a donkey.
Donkey died, daddy cried,
Inky pinky ponky.

Oh, What a Merry Land!

Songs From Around the World

We have always been fascinated by the way different peoples have expressed their cultures through music. Here is a grab bag of singing songs, dancing songs, walking songs, counting songs, loving songs, posing songs, tall tale songs, stone-passing songs and make-up-your-own-verses songs from the Caribbean, Ghana, Latin America, Spain, Great Britain, Newfoundland and the United States. Happy travels, and have a merry time.

Hail to Britannia

Here is a new way to sing some old nursery rhymes. Try *Mary Had a Little Lamb* or *Jack and Jill*. Just drop the rhymes into the song — they'll fit perfectly! It's nice to do this song standing up and marching in place on the *Hail to Britannia* chorus. By the way, "penny a loafy, taste before you buy" refers to the cry of the ice-cream vendors in the streets of London a long time ago.

England

1. Hump - ty Dump - ty sat on the wall,
all the King's hors-es and all the King's men

Hump - ty Dump - ty had a great fall sing-in'
could-n't put Hump-ty to-geth-er a - gain sing-in' "Oh, what a mer-ry land is

Eng - land." ___ And mer-ry land is Eng - land."

Brown Girl in the Ring

This West Indian children's game became a pop hit some years back. It also sounds great with just a gaggle of kids, playing and sashaying around the school yard.

With a lively Caribbean beat

West Indian singing game

1. There's a brown girl in the ring, Tra la la la la, There's a brown girl in the ring, Tra la la la la la, Brown girl in the ring, Tra la la la la, for she looks like a sug-ar and a plum, plum, plum. plum, plum, plum.

2. Skip across the ocean, Tra la la la la la...
3. Show me your motion, Tra la la la la la...
4. Wheel and spin a partner, Tra la la la la la...

104

How to play:

There are many ways to sing and play this game from Jamaica, but we like this way best. Form a circle, with one person in the middle.

In verse 1: The girl or boy in the middle skips around the circle while the players sing and clap.

In verse 2: The child skips back and forth across the middle of the circle ("skip across the ocean"). The players sing and clap.

In verse 3: In the middle of the circle, the child moves her body any way she wants to the rhythm of the song, while the other players copy.

In verse 4: The child chooses someone from the circle as a partner and they go to the middle and dance around together holding both hands, or hook elbows and swing around. They then change places. The partner becomes the child in the ring and the original child joins the circle. If a large group is playing, more than one child can be in the middle at one time.

Che Che Koolay

This chant comes from Africa, where the children sing and play it as a follow-the-leader game. We are told the words mean something like "If you're out in the ocean on your boat, return quickly, rain is coming."

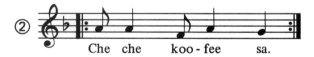

How to play:

Find parts 1, 2, 3, 4 and 5 in the song. Choose a leader. The leader faces the group and begins by singing part 1 while freezing into a statue pose. The group copies the pose as they echo the words.

The leader does this for parts 2, 3 and 4, changing the pose each time, and the group copies and echoes. During part 5, the leader and group sit flat on the floor and the group freezes. The leader gets up and walks around, trying to catch someone who is moving — even just a little bit. That person is the next leader.

Tingalayo

M' donkey short, m' donkey long, m' donkey love to sing this song! (And you will, too.)

Calypso

mf

Chorus:

Ting - a - lay - o,   run, m' lit - tle don - key, run! Ting - a - lay - o,   run m' lit - tle don - key,

2. M' donkey walk, m' donkey talk,
   M' donkey eat with a knife and fork.
   (*repeat both lines*)

   Chorus

3. M' donkey laugh, m' donkey cry,
   M' donkey love peanut butter pie.
   (*repeat*)

   Chorus

4. You can sing this slow, you can sing this
      fast,
   You can sing this sittin' on the grass.
   (*repeat*)

   Chorus

The verses are sung in echo fashion, and the chorus is sung together. Make up some new verses and choose two groups, one to sing the first two lines, the other to echo them.

107

El Sereno

In Spain and Latin America, some neighborhoods hire a private watchman whose duty it is to patrol the area during the night. He sings out the hours of the night — in the manner of "Eleven o'clock and all's well." This song comes from Extremadura in Spain and is perfect for learning to count to ten in Spanish.

Lilting waltz

Spanish counting song from Extremadura

1. El se - re - no de mi ca - lle tien - e - u - na voz muy bo - ni - ta. Que cuan - do can - ta las ho - ras, pa - re - ce u - na se - ño -

2. El sereno de mi calle
   Es un valiente embustero,
   Me ha dicho que estaba raso,
   Y ha amanecído lloviendo.

Translation:

1. The watchman on my street has a lovely voice,
   When he sings, it sounds like a young
   woman.

Ch: Watchman who sings, tell me what time it is.
   It has already sounded one o'clock, two and
      three,
   Four o'clock, five, six, seven,
   Eight, nine, ten o'clock,
   Watchman who sings, tell me what time it is.

2. The watchman on my street is a big liar,
   He said it was clear, but at dawn came the
      rain.

Stone Games

From around the world, here are three different stone-passing games. Find yourself a lovely stone and paint it, smooth it or leave it as is. Then pass it around the circle to the rhythm of the words.

Al Citron

O = pick-up
X = pass

Slow and steady

Latin America

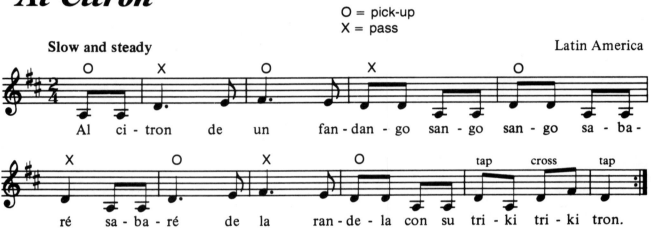

Al ci - tron de un fan - dan - go san - go san - go sa - ba -

ré sa - ba - ré de la ran - de - la con su tri - ki tri - ki tron.

How to play stone games:

Sit in a circle, cross-legged, and put your stone on the floor in front of you. Sing each song until you are familiar with it, keeping a strong beat by patting your knees. Then try this: pat your own knees, then pat to the left — put your right hand on your left knee, your left hand on your neighbor's right knee — then back to your own. We play this by passing stones to the left, so this knee pattern will help you start thinking left.

When you think you are ready, place your stone on the floor in front of your legs and follow this pattern. (It's also written above the music.):

Repeat the passing pattern for all the words in the song. Remember to pass and pick up with your right hand. Each pass and pickup falls right on the beat, as marked for each song.

If your stone has a special mark, you can tell when it comes back to you. When you can pass without losing a beat, make up your own passing patterns and try to play faster and faster.

For *Al Citron*, you use two stones, one in each hand. At the end, for "triki, triki, tron," you tap both stones on the floor, then cross them and tap, then tap again uncrossed.

Al ci-	*-tron de*	*un fan-*	*-dango sango*	*sango…*
Pick up your stone (o).	Pass stone to your neighbor on the left, placing it on the floor in front of his legs (x).	Pick up stone in front of you (o).	Pass (x).	Pick up (o).

Obwisana

("Oh, Grandma, I just hurt my finger on a rock.")

Lively   Ghana

Ob - wi - sa - na   sa - na - na,   Ob - wi - sa - na   sa.

Ob - wi - sa - na   sa - na - na,   Ob - wi - sa - na   sa.

Me Stone

Brightly   Trinidad and Tobago

Me   stone   is   me   stone,   Miss   Ma - ry.

Me   stone   is   me   stone,   Miss   Ma - ry.   Me   stone   is   me

stone,   Miss   Ma - ry.   Pass   'em down   is   me   stone,   Miss   Ma - ry.

Lots of Fish in Bonavist' Harbour

Newfoundland is an island covered with forests and surrounded by the sea, a place where people have traditionally worked as loggers and fishermen. Many Newfoundlanders are of Irish stock and their music shows it. Old-country songs are widely sung, and there is a wealth of vigorous and comical homemade songs, such as this one.

Newfoundland jig

Brightly

1. Lots of fish in Bon - a - vist' Har - bour, Lots of fish right in a - round here. Boys and girls are fish - in' to - geth - er, For - ty - five from Car - bon-ear oh, — Catch a - hold this one, catch a - hold that one,

Chorus:

swing a - round this one, swing a - round she. Dance a - round this one,

dance a - round that one, did - dle - um this one, did - dle - um dee.

Oh!

2. Uncle George got up in the mornin',
   He got up in a wonderful tear.
   He ripped the seat right out of his britches,
   Now he's got no pair to wear.
   Chorus

3. Sally is the pride of Cat Harbour,
   Ain't been swung since way last year,
   Since she met the feller from Fortune,
   What was down here fishin' last year.
   Chorus

Three Craw

This silly song tells what happened to three ''craw'' (crows) who sat upon ''a wa' '' (wall).

Brightly

Scottish folk song

Three craw sat up-on a wa', sat up-on a wa',

sat up-on a wa' - a' - a' - a'. Three craw

sat up-on a wa' on a cold and frost-y morn - ing, on a

cold and frost-y morn - ing. The
1.

morn - ing.
2.

2. The first craw couldna' find his ma...

3. The second craw fell and broke his jaw...

4. The third craw ate the other twa (two)...

5. The fourth craw wasna' there at a'...

6. And that's all I heard about the craw,
Heard about the craw, heard about the
craw-aw-aw-aw,
That's all I heard about the craw,
On a cold and frosty mornin',
On a cold and frosty mornin'.

Un Elefante

Here is a Spanish version of *One Elephant, Deux Éléphants*. We've heard a Japanese version, as well.

Latin feel

Latin America

Un e-le-fan-te se ba-lan-cea-ba so-bre la te-la de una a-ra - ña. Co -mo ve- í - a que re-sis- tí - a, fue a lla-mar un ca-ma- ra - da. -ra - da.

2. Dos elefantes se balanceaban
   Sobre la tela de una araña.
   Como veían que resestía
   Fueron a llamar un camarada.

Translation:
1. An elephant was balancing upon a spider's web.
   When he saw that it was strong enough
   He went to call a friend.

2. Two elephants were balancing…

3. Three elephants were balancing…

You can count as many elephants as you have children; counting in Spanish from one to ten is easy to learn and to pronounce:

One — un (una)	six — seis
two — dos	seven — siete
three — tres	eight — ocho
four — cuatro	nine — nueve
five — cinco	ten — diez

You can play the elephant game with this song by swinging one hand as a trunk in front of your nose and the other behind your back as a tail. Call another elephant to join you by latching his "trunk" onto your "tail."

Jack Was Every Inch a Sailor

This song of the sea is one of Newfoundland's many comic "tall tales."

Newfoundland

Brightly

Chorus:

Jack was ev - 'ry inch a sail - or.

Five and twen - ty years a whal_____ er.

Jack was ev - 'ry inch a sail - or, He was

born up - on the bright blue sea._____ 1. Now 'tis

twen - ty - five or thir - ty years since Jack first saw the light, He came in - to this

world of woe one dark and storm-y night. He was born on board his

fa-ther's ship as she was ly-ing to, 'Bout twen-ty-five or thir-ty miles south-

D.C. al Coda

east of Bac-ca-lieu. Oh,

Coda

sea, that's true!

2. When Jack grew up to be a man
   He went to Labrador.
   He fished at Indian Harbour,
   Where his father fished before.
   On his returning in the fog he met a heavy
       gale,
   Poor Jack was swept into the sea and
       swallowed by a whale.
                           Chorus

3. That whale went straight for Baffin Bay
   'Bout ninety miles an hour.
   And every time he'd blow a spray,
   He'd send it in a shower.
   "Oh, now," said Jack unto himself,
   "I must see what he's about."
   So he grabbed that whale all by the tail,
   And turned him inside out!
                           Chorus

Precious Friends

Pete Seeger is a man whose life is inseparable from his music. All of us have been influenced by his social conscience and his musical style. This song, which he wrote in 1974, reflects Pete's steadfast commitment to seeking ways by which people can achieve peace and harmony.

Inspired by the song and its message, Sharon's husband, Joe, wrote a wonderful counter-melody that makes the whole song as exhilarating to sing as the message it carries. This makes a terrific song for choirs young and old.

Music and lyrics by Pete Seeger
Countermelody by Joe Hampson

singing in har - mo - ny, Pre - cious friends, you will be there.

Skinnamarink

A piano duet arranged for four hands on one piano.

Still, after all these years, the sweetest love song we know.

PIANO I

Skin-na-ma-rin - ky din - ky dink,
skin-na-ma-rin - ky doo,
I love you.
Skin-na-ma-rin - ky din - ky dink, skin-na-ma-rin - ky doo,
I love
you.
I love you in the morn - ing, and in the af - ter-noon,
I
love you in the even - ing un-der-neath the moon.
Skin-na-ma-rin - ky din - ky dink,

PIANO II

Light soft-shoe

Skin-na-ma-rin - ky din - ky dink,

skin-na-ma-rin - ky doo, I love you.

Skin-na-ma-rin - ky din - ky dink, skin-na-ma-rin - ky doo, I love

you. I love you in the morn-ing, and in the af - ter-noon, I

love you in the even - ing un - der-neath the moon. Skin-na-ma-rin - ky din - ky dink,

Index to Titles and First Lines

Music Credits

"Hey Dum Diddeley Dum" by Marc Stone © 1979 Pachyderm Music. Used by permission.

"Michaud." Traditional, English translation by Alan Mills © Berandol Music. Used by permission.

"Precious Friends" by Pete Seeger © 1974, 1982 by Stormking Music Inc. All rights reserved. Used by permission.

"Riding Along" ("Singing a Cowboy Song") by Margaret I. Fletcher and Margaret C. Denison © 1957 by Gordon V. Thompson Music, a division of Canada Publishing Corporation, Toronto, Canada. Used by permission.

"The Very Best Band" by Joe Hampson © 1980 Pachyderm Music. Used by permission.

"Waddaly Atcha" ("Doodle Doo Doo") by Art Kassel, Mel Stitzel and Ted Morse © 1924, Renewed 1952 Leo Feist, Inc. Rights assigned to SBK Catalogue Partnership. All rights controlled and administered by SBK Feist Catalog, Inc. and Edwin H. Morris & Co., Inc. International copyright secured. All rights reserved. Used by permission.